I0109033

# Harmonica

# Harmonica

## Poems by

## Cecele Allen Kraus

*Liquid Light Press*

*Premium Chapbook First Edition*

Copyright © 2014 by Cecele Allen Kraus

ISBN-10: 0988307286

ISBN-13: 978-0-9883072-8-5

All rights reserved. Except for brief passages quoted in newspaper, magazine, radio, television or online reviews, no part of this book may be reproduced in any form or by any means, electronic or mechanical, including photocopying, scanning and recording, or by information storage or retrieval systems, without permission in writing from the Author.

# Liquid Light Press

*poetry that speaks to the heart*

*www.liquidlightpress.com*

Cover Art by Beth Thielen
Cover Design by M. D. Friedman
(*www.mdfriedman.com*)
Photo of Poet by Kevin Draves

# Contents

Bareback ...................................................................................... 1

Turnabout ................................................................................... 2

Pinetucky Baptist Singing School ......................................... 4

    i. ............................................................................................. 4

    ii. ............................................................................................ 5

    iii. ........................................................................................... 6

    iv. ........................................................................................... 7

    v. ............................................................................................ 8

    vi. ........................................................................................... 9

    vii ......................................................................................... 10

    viii. ...................................................................................... 11

    ix. ......................................................................................... 12

    x. .......................................................................................... 13

    xi. ......................................................................................... 14

    xii. ........................................................................................ 15

    xiii. ....................................................................................... 16

Soul Map .................................................................................. 17

What We Say ........................................................................... 18

Ghost Riders in the Sky ....................................................... 19

Turning Point .......................................................................... 20

Curbside 1954 ........................................................................ 22

Falling ....................................................................................... 23

Harmonica ............................................................................... 25

Three Petals ............................................................................. 26

*About the Author* ................................................................... 29

To Jerry, Andrew, Janine and Joe, Alice and Emily

**Bareback**

A stranger entered my yard on a horse as I stood barefoot with nothing to do. The rider dismounted and offered to let me ride. I jumped at the chance to leave my house with four rooms for the six of us, a broken window with cardboard replacing it, the emptiness of a scorching day with no plans except a swim at the Queen City Pool. Our street edged up to the all-black Druid High School where on Friday nights Daddy, pulled by race music, walked me over to hear the marching band play Chuck Berry's *Roll Over Beethoven,* and then, Bo Diddley's *Who Do You Love?* The drum major strutted the field. Daddy's hands twitched and slacked as he leaned into the beat, then pulled back — white skin sheened by humidity, blue eyes lit crazily in stadium lights. I had seen his fire before, and heat sent me down a Micaville road to the black Baptist Church where male quartets sang of heaven and home — soundtrack of his red clay childhood.

Somehow I mounted. The horse quivered, then galloped to the two-lane highway. Scared stiff, having only ridden my Grandpapa Allen's mules, I shot a glance down the horizon and jumped off. Now a fresh scar inches along my collar bone and reminds me of that first mark — a curvy arch over my left eyebrow, quite graceful, if you don't mind its livid red. The old scar's color comes back with age, and that urge to ride an unknown horse still flares up from time to time.

## Turnabout

With halting steps Papa Allen
walked me to a ghost town
he said once had the largest population
in Alabama. I thought perhaps
he had it wrong. I was young
and couldn't imagine such a turnabout
right in Micaville with its scattered
houses of cotton farmers and share-
croppers, one church for whites,
another for blacks, and a general store,
but Arbacoochee lives in mining ledgers
and in the mouths of storytellers
along with Chulafinnee, Wesobulga
and Crooked Creek — gold mining
towns on Cleburne County's
Piedmont Uplift.

Does the red soil
remember that swift influx
of South Carolina diggers, tent
dwellers and shack settlers
seeking escape from famine
in moon whisperings and lovers'
trysts on hill ridges? In Arbacoochee alone
settlers built saloons, general stores,
a racetrack, school, churches,
hotels and one-hundred houses —

structuring the future — dug
right into the nitty gritty for gold,
but when it was found in California,
nothing held. They left in droves
before the Yankees came.
Why did he want me to see
Arbacoochee's scraped rocks
and random planks before he died?
What did he want me to know —
that a poor county notorious for whiskey
could have such a speculative history?
Reformed bootlegger and self-proclaimed
*sinner saved by grace,*
Papa taught me what he knew —
look for those things you can't see.

## Pinetucky Baptist Singing School

i.

Intervals with no melisma
notes punching the flap flap
of wash on the line
the cotton sack's heft, the tedium
of the chicken feed bucket.

Itinerant musicians
crisscrossing Alabama back roads
led all day singings on the church grounds
and taught Daddy to read
shape note music.

A sepia-toned photograph
reveals him, a skinny blue-eyed youth
among cousins and neighbors
head thrown back, hands
beating out time,

*This world is not my home.*

ii.

Falsetto voices chilled
the women — opened their ears

to long-dead babies' cries.
In the rafters ghosts railed.

Old men dozed as girls tossed off
bonnets in sunlit pine thickets.

Fervent young men — guns left at home
stamped the wood floors

and caught up in raw music
ceased fighting.

Daddy swore
he'd leave Pinetucky behind.

iii.

Grandmother Allen dreamed
Daddy at the altar

and told Brother Holmes, the traveling
preacher, she'd had a vision
as real as the cows she milked.

*He'll grow up to be a preacher.*

Shadowed by his mother's hope,
Daddy dreamed me playing the piano
and called it a vision, as real

as the Mason and Hamlin upright
he bought for a hundred dollars

scratched up, with ivories missing
around middle C — a stool that swirled.

I made his dream my own.

iv.

Daddy wore a patrolman uniform
with a belt wide enough

for a holster and gun
its brass buckle level with my eyes.

Leaving the house angry
he didn't even hug me goodbye.

In housecoat and slippers
hair still in pin curls, Mother peered

out the window, wiped tears
on her sleeve and said,

*look what you've done.*
*He'll never come back.*

That daddy's gone — that tall, strong
daddy — never had a cold

in his life. The daddy who lived on
died early of cancer —

brain rattled, muscles slack
his demons dispersed like startled crows.

v.

Daddy's hands pummeled
my head, shoulders and arms —
no way to break free.

My best friend Gloyce and I giggled
in the back pew —
just couldn't stop ourselves.

From the choir loft and down
the aisle, he grew larger and larger until
he grabbed my arm — pulled me outside.

*Get in the car,* he yelled, *we're going home.*

Gloyce ran through fireflies and tumbleweeds
barking dogs and the prefabs
of our paltry neighborhood.

Maybe that was the last time he hit me
the last time he said,

*This hurts me more
than it hurts you.*

I was eight years old.
How could he know

how much I hurt?

vi.

The stadium blazed. Crimson clad players

cheerleaders and majorettes

all under the gaze of Bear Bryant

in plaid fedora, cuff links and vest.

Daddy asked me to the game —

just the two of us — twenty minutes

and worlds away from our spare

campus bungalow. What could I wear?

Hand-me-downs puddled on my closet floor.

I knew college girls dressed for homecoming —

fur-trimmed suits with pencil skirts

feather hats and alligator pumps.

*You're a child,* Mother said, *just wear*

*any dress. That orange one sets off*

*your red hair nicely.* Daddy said, *You'll be*

*Technicolor when you're old enough*

*to wear lipstick.*

vii.

Dusty bins filled the back room
of Lively Music Service.

Cedric Flowers, the blind tuner, presided over
worn pianos and Hammond organs.

I listened as he struck each hammer
over and over, up and down the keyboard

turning pegs to an accurate pitch
until his hands released

into free-fall melodies.
Cedric knew how to play by ear.

A regular customer, Daddy searched
for music I could play and found Handel

and Bach on cream-colored sheets
trimmed with black filigree.

In return, I mapped the contours
of his voice, memorized the veins

and scarred terrain of his hands,
flex of his forearms signaling tempo.

What I knew was how to follow
the beat as Daddy led a choir

of untrained singers.

viii.

A baritone shaped smooth
in the precipices and hollows

of Pinetucky's music, honed by songs
from an ancient hymnal

notes shaped into diamonds
ovals, rectangles and triangles.

Daddy never fully lost the sound
of that emphatic singing.

In that world anyone could sing
anyone could lead — *O who*

*will come and go with me?*
*I am on my journey home* —

four part harmonies
a cappella renderings

full-throated outpourings
like crows mourning.

ix.

Mother never drank
or smoked cigarettes

wore flowered print dresses
her slip often showed.

Stepping from choir loft to pulpit
she joined Daddy in duets

and with a voice as jagged as Kitty Wells'
sang of green pastures

lions lying down
with lambs — fought off

the honky-tonk angels
and cheating hearts hiding

in her low tones, kept sin
and pride at bay — but not desire.

Sheepishly, eyes askance
she slipped a hand in her bodice

tugged her bra strap into place.

x.

In a long crinkled black and white photograph
Daddy poses with one-hundred tuxedoed men.
A grin offsets his body honed lean in cotton fields.
Somewhere on the Illinois Central between Birmingham
and Chicago or on the North Coast Limited to Pasco
he became a stranger in a strange land,
and in the shadow of Hanford's towers,
policed atomic energy workers made mad
by loneliness and beer — welders, carpenters,
construction crewmen — poor men from Oklahoma
and Missouri with skills useful for bomb building.

In the bar he'd open a hose to stun drunks off to bed.
Quartet harmonies quieted him until Mother and I
reached the Pasco station. When classical music called
he joined a chorus touring the Northwest. By then
he'd settled in Richland, a town pasted and thrown
on a desert landscape right along where the Snake
and Columbia rivers meet. We three came together
in a thin-walled prefab with no basement
or attic.

xi.

At Red O'Donnell's house, Daddy
sang four-part harmony with friends

rehearsed *Have a Little Talk with Jesus*
to sing on Richland radio

dreamed Pinetucky Baptist Church
deacons swaggering in Sunday suits

wives cooled by cardboard fans
stapled to thin wood sticks

Jones Funeral Parlor on one side
Jesus gently smiling on the other.

We sat on the piano bench
Daddy's deep voice vibrating —

*why    don't    you*
*tell Him all about your troubles?*

The tenor took the high notes —
*He will answer by and by —*

and finally, all together,
*just a little talk with Jesus makes it right.*

They let me play the piano for rehearsals —
I was eight years old. So badly

I wanted to keep up. Daddy said,
*When we move back to Alabama*

*you'll have to play faster.*

xii.

Intimacies passed between us in our Chevy — oranges sectioned and counted out, bologna on white bread passed around, saltines nibbled. Sometimes Coca-Colas or Juicy Fruit gum. Cargo-laden trucks shuddered our car. Arizona heat glinted the highway. For 3,000 miles Mother changed Philip's diapers in the moving car. Carefully guarded in the ruckus, an Ivory soap bar with a gun and holster, tennis racquet and Bible carved into it — Daddy's going away gift sculpted by his buddy, Lee Casebolt.

*Don't bump that package*, Mother said. Jammed in with supplies, Anna and I just couldn't stop wiggling. With no more books to read, I whined, *Are we there yet?* So fast he hit me, I didn't see it coming. Daddy reached his arm right over the back seat — didn't even swerve. A whack. Mother gasped, cuddled the baby close. Anna curled into her pillow. Out the window I saw a Hopi family hitchhiking — the girl about my age, a baby on her mother's back — wind whipping their straight black hair.

xiii.

My brother didn't see his silent cues
from the pulpit — Daddy's finely tuned messages —
turn of head, shift in posture.

*I always thought you were in charge*
*of when he ended the service.*

While Daddy preached, I waited
in the first pew, close to the piano.

Rarely missing shifts in his voice, staying
right with him, I slipped from pew
to piano bench

and as I sat down, he made the altar call —
*just as I am without one plea* —
a private choreography.

Leaving out hard notes, I struck
only those needed for safe passage.

## Soul Map

A baby in my arms, another child

buried in Pinetucky's red clay.

At the Birmingham station

my childless sisters pass her back and forth.

Dark presence in funeral coat and veiled hat,

Mother slips me a white Bible.

As the train crosses Mississippi, I unzip it.

Ruth joins me for 3,000 miles to Pasco

where my husband has gone to work.

Hagar wanders the desert with her child.

John the Baptist, honed by honey

and locusts, skirts the Dakota bluffs.

All accompany me through prairie

and tumbleweed drift.

Steadying myself I breathe the train's wail.

A fellow traveler says, *Chinooks*

*in these regions blow overnight*

*melting snow on tablelands and river basins.*

Maybe this terrain will thaw my heart.

No choking kudzu here, no magnolia scent.

I trace the landscape of death,

flame the ashes of desire.

## What We Say

Now far from doctors and deep
in Cleburne County, Mother keened.

Her three-year-old boy was pallid
burning with fever.

Grandmama Carr said, *I'll take care of
the boy. No need for a doctor.*

My Grandmother said that, even though
she had lost her eight-year-old son

when she was a young mother —
hit by a careening car.

Over rutted roads, Daddy drove them
to the hospital past houses of relatives critical

of Mother's city ways. Her womb carried me
as she buried her firstborn

and while grief made her mindless
I drew nourishment within her.

In that soil I was born, and, yes, she held me
tried to find his smell in my soft clothes

joy in my red curls, but shadowed always
by her three-year-old boy.

I was born in red clay
watered with tears from an infinite well

left to ponder what we say
when we say goodbye.

**Ghost Riders in the Sky**

Words opened our Chevy, pierced
with possibilities. Daddy sang along

with the Sons of the Pioneers
as we crossed the Black Warrior bridge.

I saw those tortured beasts
*red-eyed cows in the devil's herd*

that roamed mesas and died
doomed to forever roll the heavens

cattle possessed by spirits of cowboys
punished for unrepentance, banished

to stampeding herds. Daddy and I
didn't talk much, but music bound us —

*He Shall Feed His Flock* and plain hymns
such as *We're Marching to Zion.*

Did Daddy see what I saw?
Did he repent? Mourn?

At our usual diner the tinny jukebox
played Buddy Holly's *Come along*

*and be my party doll.* I dropped in a quarter
to hear it six more times

singing along all by myself.

**Turning Point**

In the very spot where farmers
once gathered at Charlie Wade's store

rusted cargo containers jut
and angle like giant

Erector Sets, their cabs
disconnected

and dying in some distant locale.
Red bricks, ubiquitous sign

of Southern modernity, replace
rough planks of the Baptist church.

Micaville is a crossroads with little
to recommend it.

Memory adds weight
to such a place. Love scans

for details. Here my grandmother
kept a shotgun at the door

to scare roustabouts
looking for her boys.

*She hath done what she could,*
testifies her tombstone.

A corrugated metal autobody
offers car and truck repair

to children of farmers who knew
how to fix their own machines.

In a faded corner house, I can almost see
blue-eyed Uncle Theo by his barber

chair, scissors in hand, shadowed
by a dangling lightbulb glow.

Hard to know what will be there next — café
or Laundromat — dreams come

and go. When his plan for escape
from farming failed, he moved

to Orange Beach, the Gulf's
Redneck Riviera, and cut

the hair of tourists.

## Curbside 1954

Whenever we drove through Birmingham
I looked for Sloss Mines — red steel
pouring down chutes, ore plumbed
under a delirium of smoking towers,
steel mill families in shotgun shanties
with porches tacked on like sharecropper shacks.
Antidote to *my* Tuscaloosa, row after row
of tenuous pastel houses. Church services
like set pieces crafted to avoid surprise.
White-gloved girls, permed mothers,
starched fathers. I wanted gritty and raw.
Street people going nowhere I could see —
a drunk grabbing a woman's breast,
her raucous laugh. Men in fedoras
smoking cigarettes in phone booths.

A dark-skinned man in night-colored
clothes stumbled off the curb.
When we hit him Daddy jumped out,
laid hands on his injured shoulder, called down
God's power, awaited the cop's siren.
Children unsure of our trip's next leg,
not yet could we see what our father shared
with this steelworker — a red clay world
of well water boiled for baths, outhouses
on cold nights, plowed fields abandoned
for industrial toil, blacks and whites
living together yet worlds apart.
What lured him were chance encounters —
a man thrown in his path. After that accident
Daddy pulled up to the steelworker's curb,
knocked, crossed over his wooden threshold
every time he passed through Birmingham,
and now, in a drive-through world,
I hunger after that past.

## Falling

Raised in hills where fighting was manly, my father's hands quieted only after he was fired at the state mental hospital for threatening to hit another chaplain. Jobless except for churches where he preached twice a month, he tried to make money selling World Book encyclopedias. When diagnosed with prostate cancer, he put away dark suits, starched shirts and ties, and wore polyester shirts in geometric patterns with wash and wear slacks in pale blue, dove grey, and avocado green, though he still polished his shoes on Saturdays with paste from a tin with a metal turner on the side. Until his strength gave out, he challenged students for pick-up tennis at the university courts — a game he learned after leaving Cleburne County where football was elemental. He won every time, but we put our battles aside, drinking Mountain Dew on the car ride home.

~~~

Mother always said, there are two things you can't skimp on — dental care and shoes, and referred to her own gum disease as pyorrhea, as if a scientific name would take away the shame. Somehow she found money to buy us sturdy shoes, and I polished my penny loafers carefully, using Daddy's leather polish, brush, and felt cloth. Somehow Daddy found ways to buy suits, ties, shirts, and good shoes, working out payment plans with Tuscaloosa's Jewish merchants, much to Mother's dismay. Returning home from New York with bagels from Murray's on Bleecker Street, I wore expensive sunglasses, looking for admiration. My father picked me up at the airport in a red second-hand Skylark, slightly rusted and cluttered with debris. Though accustomed to a shabby house, I was startled by his fall from elegance and downcast eyes — a button missing, shoes scuffed. I took off my fancy shades.

~~~

From his recliner, Daddy made games for his grandchildren, popping his dentures in and out as they squealed. As tennis became impossible he cast about for things to do, took up gardening despite his hatred for farming. Sitting on a stool to save his aching joints he edged along the rows he'd planted, deadheading and snipping his small crop of tomatoes and pole beans. He had all afternoon to finish.

~~~

He didn't tell his doctor of difficult erections. When he did, it was too late. He journeyed to Oklahoma to have Oral Roberts lay hands on him, then turned to Laetrile, the sixties' magic cancer cure. Reconciling himself to death, he sat with Mother's prayer group, eyes closed as Effie strummed plaintively — prayed as sunlight spilled over him, *I know, Lord, You won't give me more pain than I can bear.*

~~~

Dipped in ice cubes, bone-chilled, was his pain more than he could bear? Relief came with daylight. Mother washed his ruined body, lotioned his hands, combed his wispy hair and turned him. Without gagging, I washed his dentures, gently easing them into his mouth just before he slipped into a coma.

## Harmonica

Daddy requested a harmonica — instrument
of his childhood. Blind now from the spread
of cancer, he needed me to drive him
to the music store.

With one hand I steered him, picked up
my toddler son with the other.
Daddy's arm trembled in my grasp
while Andrew grabbed my sunglasses.

The owner greeted him. *B.W. Allen,
I know you! I know your people over in
Cleburne County.* Hands that had struck me
caressed the small silver instrument

and putting it to his mouth, he played
*Jimmy cracked corn and I don't care, Jimmy
cracked corn and I don't care, Jimmy cracked corn
and I don't care, my master's gone away.*
Andrew shouted out, *Again!*

Having never met a stranger,
Daddy's face shone. Who was he
at that late moment, a man sucked hollow
by cancer or a man playing old songs
into the universe?

## Three Petals

Stars of Bethlehem, May's
tiniest white flowers, lead

to the clove over rocks
made treacherous by Biblical rains.

Pale trilliums, three-petaled — maybe God
the Father, Son, and Holy Ghost —

cluster on stream banks,
but I'm asymmetrical. Nerves

shoot from right clavicle to mid-back
forearm to thumb —

I pass my hiking pole
hand to hand to stave off muscle pain.

A slab bridge over a stream engorged
by meltwater, a mile or so of flat — then up.

Rocks jut. A crevasse cracks
deep in the mountain wall.

When I was a child, if you dug
deep enough you'd reach China.

If you sang *We are climbing Jacob's ladder*
the sky would open. Up in the clouds

down to the earth's bowels — *world
without end. Amen.*

I wedge my left boot
onto an outcrop —

one hand grasps a root, the other
braces for leverage —

then hoist my weight
onto the craggy ledge.

Song won't help me.
Beyond trilliums

I arrive to where
talus and rubble tip

at odd angles. Boulders cast off
by Taconic upthrust erode

into soup pots and teakettles,
and my body, taxed, recollects

falling, a clavicle rebuilt
with a steel plate. May I dwell

in this Catskills hubbub —
sensorium of chaos.

## About the Author

Cecele Allen Kraus is a former psychotherapist, and author of two poetry chapbooks: *Dreaming Barranquilla* and *Tuscaloosa Bypass.* Her work has appeared in *Naugatuck River Review, Up the River, riverbabble, The Avocet, Passager, Chronogram, Windfall, Backstreet, The Literary Gazette, News and Reviews* (National Psychological Association for Psychoanalysis newsletter), the Returned Peace Corps Volunteers to Colombia newsletter, and in two chapbook anthologies — *Zephyrs* and *Java Wednesdays.* Cecele lives in Copake, New York, where she loves to walk the trails of the Taconic Range.

*Credits and Acknowledgements*

Poems in this chapbook previously appeared in the following
publications:

>"Bareback" (earlier version), The River Reporter in *The Literary
>Gazette*
>
>"Curbside," *Zephyrs,* Vol. 6, Millay Press
>
>"Soul Map," *Zephyrs,* Vol. 6, Millay Press
>
>"Pinetucky Baptist Singing School" (section ix), *Up the River*
>
>"Ghost Riders in the Sky," *Up the River (*online edition)

**Other Books by Cecele Allen Kraus**

*Dreaming Barranquilla* (The Troy Book Makers 2009)

*Tuscaloosa Bypass* (Finishing Line Press 2011)

*Other Books from Liquid Light Press*

All Liquid Light Press books are available directly from *liquidlightpress.com* or from any of the current major global distribution channels including Amazon, Barnes and Noble, the iBookstore and the Ingram Catalog.

*Leaning Toward Whole*, **Poems by M. D. Friedman (Released June, 2011)**
This poetry chapbook from the international award winning poet, M. D. Friedman, contains pieces both poignant and personal.

*The Miracle Already Happening – Everyday Life with Rumi,* **Poems by Rosemerry Wahtola Trommer (Released December, 2011)**
Rosemerry Wahtola Trommer's superb collection of poems, inspired by Rumi, is full of heart, humor, peace and wisdom.

*Spiral,* **Poems by Lynda La Rocca (Released March, 2012)**
Award winning poet, Lynda La Rocca, creates a compelling poetic and melodic discourse from the persistent cravings and fears inside of each of us.

*From the Ashes,* **Poems by Wayne A. Gilbert (Released June , 2012)**
Master jazz Sufi poet, Wayne A. Gilbert, chronicles the loss of his mother with powerful, bittersweet honesty and poignant expression universal in its scope, transcendent in its depth of understanding and exquisitely musical in form.

*ah,* **Poems by Rachel Kellum (Released July, 2012)**
Rachel Kellum's *ah* is a transparent poetic odyssey into the ethereal that is both provocative and inspirational.

*Catalyst,* **Poems by Jeremy Martin (Released December, 2012)**
Jeremy Martin's *Catalyst* is a mind field of delight.

*Of Eyes and Iris,* **Poems by Erika Moss Gordon (Released March, 2013)**
Erica Moss Gordon's *Of Eyes and Iris* shines with the purity of a mountain stream, dances with sunlight, and shivers with the chill of perception.

*Your House Is Floating,* **Poems by Susan Whitmore (Released June, 2013)**
Susan Whitmore's craft is as smooth, crisp and satisfying as olive oil on fresh garden greens.

*Nowhere Near Morning,* **Poems by Jeffrey M. Bernstein (Released October 2013)**
Jeffery Bernstein speaks directly to his readers in a poetic voice that is both raspy and wise. His poetry grabs you where you live, knocks on your door and invites you out to ponder the meaning of life at the local pub.

www.ingramcontent.com/pod-product-compliance
Lightning Source LLC
Chambersburg PA
CBHW021915040426
42447CB00007B/871